WHAT NEXT?

...and other recent cartoons by

Including the Tanzanian journal and sketchbook

This book is dedicated to Solomon Buster,
the kid who squeezed the Prime Minister's nose.

Thanks to all involved: Mary Hughson, Janet Hughson, Desmond Morton, Gaëtan Coté and Pat Duggan.
Thanks as always to Kim McArthur and the terrific team at McArthur & Company.

WHAT NEXT?

...and other recent cartoons by

With an introduction by Desmond Morton

Text by Terry Mosher and Janet Hughson

McArthur & Company

Toronto

First published in Canada in 2006 by
McArthur & Company
322 King St. West, Suite 402
Toronto, Ontario
M5V 1J2
www.mcarthur-co.com

Library and Archives Canada Cataloguing in Publication

Aislin
        What next? : and other recent cartoons / by Aislin.

ISBN 1-55278-609-9

1. Canada--Politics and government--1993-2006--Caricatures and cartoons.
2. Canadian wit and humor, Pictorial. I. Title.

NC1449.A37A4 2006   971.07'20207   C2006-903392-7

Cover Illustration by AISLIN
Layout, Design, and Electronic Imaging by Mary Hughson
Printed and Bound in Canada by Transcontinental Printing, Inc.

The publisher would like to acknowledge the financial support of the Government of Canada through the Book Publishing Industry Development Program (BPIDP) and the Canada Council for our publishing activities. The publisher further wishes to acknowledge the financial support of the Ontario Arts Council for our publishing program.

10 9 8 7 6 5 4 3 2 1

CONTENTS

Introduction by Desmond Morton /6

Introduction

I think most of you know what's happening back there on the cover. You may even remember the event. On a post-election tour to make himself better known to his new subjects, Prime Minister Harper was offered a little boy's face for a campaign-style kiss. The alert little nipper promptly seized Harper's schnoz and gave it an agonizing twist. The lad was promptly returned to *terra firma*. Media dutifully squashed their glee of horror and recorded both the event and the P.M.'s earnest reassurances. End of story.

The photos lasted longer and a cartoon by Montreal's Terry Mosher etched the event on our memories. Voters responded with all the diversity any good cartoon provokes. "How dare a kid attack the Prime Minister. Security should have shot him." "Look at the way parents raise their children these days!" "Wish I'd done it!" "Why is Aislin recording such a disgusting stunt?" "Dear Mr. Harper took it with a smile. Maybe he's not such a jerk after all!"

I suspect Aislin saw a boy acting just like a cartoonist a little early in life. Twisting a politician's nose is a literal way of filling that box at the top of the editorial page. Maybe Mosher really grabbed the boy's point of view. Snatched from the crowd, hoisted by some PR flack to soften Harper's nerdy image, without even a "by your leave". What self-respecting child wouldn't avenge such an affront? What cartoonist, assigned to avenge the daily affronts we all suffer from the self-important and over-indulged, wouldn't recognize a fellow heckler? Terry tells me that he didn't even know the boy was known to his folks as "Buster".

Mosher has been tweaking noses for underdogs across Canada and even the world using his daughter's name Aislinn, since 1967. That's when an ex-Montrealer and fellow Georgevilllite, John Scott, slid him onto the cover of *TIME* Magazine to offer its readers an unworshipful view of Pierre Elliott Trudeau. At the time, some Canadians were quite annoyed; most were amused. Trudeau himself proceeded effortlessly to become one of our best – or one of our worst – prime ministers. After all, having his nose twisted by a kid called Buster didn't hurt Harper's prime ministership, any more than John Wilson Bengough's rude images of John A. Macdonald, George Racey's versions of Wilfrid Laurier or Normand Hudon's Mackenzie King could end their careers. All cartoonists can do is test our tolerance for free speech and, as countless textbooks testify, make the posthumous re-invention of politicians by historians a whole lot more fun for our students.

Royal Orr chats with BBC correspondent Vicky Ntetema in Dar-es-Salaam

Like most of his fellow historians, Terry Mosher knows that politics is only a small part of life, however central it becomes to some self-important fools. Like most Montrealers, Aislin's visual imagination extends to play and work (in that order), to Montreal's long winters and luscious summers, to sports and shopping, music and movies, the slope of our mountain and the depths of our potholes, not to mention the taxes we apparently pay to delay fixing them.

Beyond us, never very far way, is a Quebec of complex but soft-edged sensitivities, to which Mosher brings a sensibility seemingly denied to Torontonians and usually derided in Winnipeg, Calgary or Vancouver. Beyond Canada is a savage world that has often forced us or our ancestors to rush here for safety and a fresh start, and which often summons us back to the old quarrels – as in 1914 or 1945, or in August 2006.

This year, Terry and Mary were summoned on their own world adventure. Inspired by Montreal media veteran Royal Orr, an AIDS mission from McGill University's Health Centre invited the Moshers to share its pilgrimage to the southern highlands of Tanzania. Their visit opened their eyes as it opens this book, not merely with despair and shame, but with those qualities Terry and Mary bring to their own lives and to ours: honesty, hope and just enough wild humour to keep us from going nuts.

Yes, it is great that Bill Gates and his richest buddies have squeezed out billions of dollars to fight AIDS in Africa, but take a look at Tanzania's southern region through the Moshers' eyes and ears, and see what you can do (www.highlandshope.com). And then get back to Gomery, Wal-Mart, the Middle East, how Montreal's Expos became the team President George W. Bush now has to cheer for and much more. And check that you aren't one of the poor schmucks staring back at you over an Aislin caption. If you are, smile hard. Isn't that what Steve Harper's handlers made him do!

Desmond Morton
McGill Institute for the Study of Canada
desmond.morton@mcgill.ca

CHAPTER 1

A Tanzanian Sojourn

There was no doubt about it; we had come to the end of the road.

After plowing through the deep, brick-red mud of an increasingly narrow track for the better part of 2 hours, our small medical team was forced to turn back. For today at least, we wouldn't reach the remote location in the Tanzanian highlands where HIV-positive patients waited to see us. It was a stern lesson on the challenges of treating seriously ill people in places where there is little or no infrastructure. Even on short acquaintance, I knew our dedicated medical professionals would find it hard to abandon the effort, but then our trip to Tanzania was about finding new ways around old obstacles.

It was thanks to Royal Orr that my wife, Mary Hughson, and I had the chance to be part of this "scouting" group and to experience both the heartbreak and the hope in Tanzania's Southern Highlands.

Aida Fungo, Bulongwa

A commitment is made

Moved by what he saw while filming a documentary in Tanzania several years ago, the former CBC radio host and one-time leader of Alliance Quebec committed his networks and his energy to the fight against AIDS in Africa, especially in Tanzania.

While that country has made the battle with HIV a national priority, the medical infrastructure is fragile. Access to antiretrovirals is extremely limited, especially in rural areas.

Orr wants to help make HIV/AIDS testing and treatment more generally available, so he has built links between the McGill University Health Centre and a coalition known as the Highlands Hope Consortium (HHC): two hospitals and one HIV treatment centre in Tanzania's Njombe and Makete districts. He hopes that sharing knowledge and resources will one day yield a blueprint for an HIV-AIDS strategy that can be used all over Africa.

Since there is no better teacher than direct experience, Orr organized a trip to Tanzania in January 2006 for his McGill partners. Norbert ("Nobby") Gilmore, a veteran of Montreal's AIDS battles and a leading Canadian expert on HIV, was joined by Roy Baskind, a neurology resident with clinical and research experience in rural Zambia, and Madeleine Buck, Assistant Director of McGill's School of Nursing. Orr invited me to tag along.

Why ask a cartoonist along for the ride?

Orr wanted to create public awareness of the Makete project and asked if I would produce a journal and sketchbook. Inspired by his enthusiasm, Mary and I agreed to be part of the team.

Leaving Montreal in the grip of winter, we transited in Amsterdam and flew south. I will never forget waking from a brief sleep to a spectacular sight: the mighty Nile 30,000 feet below, twisting its way through the eastern Sahara. Passing over a very beige Khartoum, we continued south into the night before arriving in Dar es Salaam after more than 24 hours of travel, a world away from snow and ice.

Even at midnight, the darkened city was baking in heat and humidity. "Dar" is Tanzania's largest city – about the size of Montreal – and is a rapidly growing commercial centre, boasting the largest port on Africa's east coast. Next morning we boarded a 15-seater plane chartered from a South African evangelical outfit. Pilot Jan Smits, a Tin-Tin look-alike, asked Jesus to guide us safely on our journey. Even the agnostics among us bowed their heads.

Our first destination was Njombe, a transportation hub and agricultural centre in the Southern Highlands. From there, trucks and heavily laden daladala buses fan out to points throughout the region. Unfortunately, it's also a transit station for HIV/AIDS, spread by truckers and migrant workers.

Daladala bus

Breaking Taboos

Njombe's largest employer is TANWAT, the British-owned Tanganyika Wattle Company. Under the leadership of Managing Director Ronnie Cox, TANWAT has built and continues to fund a 40-bed private hospital that provides care for its employees, their families and seasonal workers.

The company also finances community outreach activities to promote prevention of HIV and help reduce the stigma attached to AIDS. The McGill team was especially struck by the work of head nurse Betty Liduke, a respected community leader who has been challenging taboos about HIV and sex for 20 years. The first nurse to receive foreign training in peer counseling, Liduke single-handedly organized outreach programs to 17 villages in the Njombe area. She is warmly greeted everywhere and villagers feel comfortable asking her for "sweeties"

– condoms. We were delighted that, thanks to support from the McGill School of Nursing and Canadian friends of Highlands Hope, she attended the August 2006 AIDS conference in Toronto.

The scourge of corruption

Leaving Njombe, we drove further into the Southern Highlands, to the tiny mountain town of Ikonda. Dirt-poor and often enveloped in clouds, the town is overlooked by a 220-bed "hospital in the sky" run by an Italian branch of the Catholic Movement of Consolata. About 70 per cent of the hospital's patients have HIV-related complaints, while its associated outpatient facility treats more than 900 HIV-positive adults.

Padre Ceschia, 82, has worked in Tanzania since 1951. These days his particular charges are children orphaned by AIDS. "Whatever you decide to do," he advised the McGill

Betty Liduke and Madeleine Buck at Tanwat hospital

team, "make sure you build a short, strong pipe between those who have and those who need. Long pipes leak."

Corruption is not a uniquely African phenomenon, of course, but it does hurt more in places like this, where every penny counts. There may be cause for some optimism in Tanzania: recently elected President Jakaya Kikwete has insisted that his ministers eliminate graft in their departments.

Waiting…

The team toured the Consolata facilities amid wry jokes about the comparative cleanliness of the complex when set against Montreal's Royal Vic. All humour vanished as Roy Baskind and head nurse Omolima Mahemge gently examined Witnesse Mwihuka, a tiny 5-year-old girl. Her mother, from whom she contracted HIV, had died of an AIDS-related illness.

This little girl personified the most painful impression I took away from my Tanzanian experience. AIDS is about waiting. Everyone waits – for money and drugs, for treatment – for death. That tiny girl was just wasting away, a bit more every day. Close by, 30-year-old Faraja Mlowe lay patiently in her hospital bed. She knew her fate. And she waited.

There is no community outreach here. Patients and their families walk many, many kilometres to attend the hospital or one of the clinics – if they can afford the nominal fee. Many cannot.

Tough choices

From Ikonda, we went on to the town of Makete, where we were received by Shadrack Manyviewa, the Lutheran bishop, who prayed for an end to the diocese's current "difficulties".

He was referring to the condition of the 80-bed Bulongwa Hospital. Once a poor but efficient institution, it has been under a

Roy Baskind examines a child

Waiting

efficient institution, it has been under a cloud since the previous administrator, a European-educated Tanzanian appointed by Bishop Manyviewa, disappeared amid murmurings of financial irregularities. Donations from Europe, the lifeblood of the hospital, are being withheld until results of an audit are released. The new administrator, Dr. Hans Reichold, must make impossibly tough choices. How should he spend the little money there is? Keep the power and water on? Pay staff? Buy proper surgical tools? The facilities are primitive: Reichold told me that a visiting German student had mistaken the hospital's operating room for a medical museum.

Reichold and his dedicated staff soldier on. Despite problems at the hospital, locals still flood there, knowing it is superior to the government-run facility, where staff may or may not show up for work.

Getting the hospital back on track would save its orphanage, although it can only house about 35 children. Sadly, there are many other children in Makete who desperately need help. In a population of just 105,000, an estimated 15,000 children have been orphaned by HIV/AIDS, the highest proportion in Tanzania. With the number of child-led households skyrocketing, primary school teachers are selflessly taking in many of their orphaned pupils. The head teacher at Bulongwa Primary School has adopted five of the school's 145 orphans, providing basic care on his salary of about $3 U.S. a day.

There is some good news regarding Bulongwa. The excellent Care and Treatment Centre (CTC) connected to the hospital is funded independently by the Lutheran Church of Austria. Run by Dr. Rainer Brandl, one of the founders of the Highlands Hope Consortium, it is accepting a growing number of patients for HIV testing and antiretrovirals.

However, both the CTC and the hospital face two major difficulties. One is old attitudes.

"Even two years ago, people kept silent on the subject of AIDS," Vicky Ntetema of the BBC told me. "If someone got sick and died, it was always attributed to something

Nobby Gilmore and Jackson Mbogela with a patient

else, maybe tuberculosis. But when outreach programs reached the villages, frank discussions about AIDS became possible."

We followed Rainer Brandl's assistant co-ordinator, Jackson Mbogela, as he toured several villages where PIUMA, a creative new outreach program, is being tested. In one such settlement, a group of people fighting the stigma of HIV/AIDS, have adopted the motto *"Pima ili uishi kwa matumaini"* – "Be tested, and live with hope." An elder told us of summoning up the courage to be tested. Discovering he was HIV-positive, he urged his wives to be tested. Two of the three were infected.

The distance to treatment centres is the other challenge. Women are especially affected, as they are both patients and caregivers. Everywhere we went in Tanzania

Student

13

PIUMA members dance

walked away from us, we read the Swahili proverb on her gaily coloured Kanga skirt: *"Atake hachoki"* - "A person in need never gets tired."

I hope to return to Tanzania one day. Despite the poverty, disease and corruption, there is great strength and dignity in the people and I feel a connection. In the meantime, I follow the work launched by Royal Orr and the McGill team. As they help with the fight against HIV/AIDS, they remain conscious of the well-intentioned mistakes of the past.

As Nobby Gilmore says, "We didn't go to Tanzania to reinvent the flat tire."

For information on how you can help, visit www.highlandshope.com. For my full journal, visit www.aislin.com.

baskets of vegetables or buckets of water, on their way to feed their children or to care for family members in hospital. I developed a deep admiration for them. In one hospital, we were introduced to a woman who, just hours earlier, had had a grossly enlarged uterus removed. Magdalena, 39, was walking around without benefit of painkillers. She explained she was needed back home soon and so, nine days later, set off to travel 100 kilometres of rough road. Magdalena's quiet determination provided another of my enduring images of Tanzania. As she

PIUMA member encourages others to be tested

Gathered under the protective PIUMA umbrella

GRANDMOTHER and CHILD

Grandmothers arise at Toronto AIDS conference…

CHAPTER 2

Canada:

You Gotta Love It

...while Stephen Harper is busy elsewhere

After our visit to Tanzania, Betty Liduke, Jackson Mbogela and Dr. Rainer Brandl returned the courtesy in August of 2006 by traveling to Toronto to attend the XVI International AIDS conference along with 25,000 other participants. Jackson's reaction to events were particularly revealing given that he had never traveled outside Tanzania, never mind ever flown on an airplane before. One of the speakers at the AIDS conference was highly critical of our own Prime Minister, Stephen Harper, for not attending the event. Jackson was genuinely puzzled that the police hadn't appeared to cart the speaker off in chains!

The Tanzanian experience led to a renewed appreciation of how fortunate we are here in Canada. In comparison to most nations around the world, we live in a diverse, progressive, wealthy and accepting country. On the other hand, let's not go over board here; H.L. Mencken did say that every decent man is ashamed of the government he lives under.

.07% OF OUR BUDGET TO HELP SAVE AFRICA?

Are Canadians as generous as they could be?

Contrast bitterly cold Januarys with…

... extremely hot Julys

Our Governor-General, a Chinese-Canadian woman steps down…

...to be replaced by a Haitian-Canadian woman

Canadian provincial demands…

O, CANADA...

...by demanding provincial Canadians

Straight press, part 1

Straight guy

Straight press, part 2

Depressed straight

Supreme Court rules in favour of gay mariage

CHAPTER 3

Ottawa:
Bytown Capers

Everyone had high expectations for Paul Martin – the "whiz kid", ex-Minister of Finance – as he took over leadership of the Liberal Party from Jean Chrétien in November 2003. Decisive and tough, Martin would surely be a strong leader for the country and stake out Canada's rightful place in the world once elected Prime Minister.

The election duly took place in June 2004. However, Martin just squeaked in with a minority government and the questions started to fly.

Would the new Prime Minister have the political will and the personal clout to aggressively clean house within the Liberal Party and the Government? There was lots of activity, but little apparent change.

Would his younger, more diverse Cabinet appeal to Canadians and inspire them with renewed trust in the Liberals? That honeymoon was soon over. Immigration Minister Judy Sgro was forced to resign in January 2005 over allegations of trading visas for services in the so-called *Strippergate* affair. Despite later being cleared of any wrong-doing, the damage had been done and the Opposition knew it.

Martin was also faced with the challenge of appeasing the NDP just enough to garner Jack Layton's ongoing support in Parliament. By throwing money at health care and other social causes, the new Government bought itself a little breathing room, but not much.

Finally, and perhaps most importantly, Martin needed to distance himself from the sins of the Chrétien era and decided to appoint Justice John Gomery to look into the sponsorship scandals. Did it work?

Well, actually… no.

Drunk reveller caught urinating on the National War Memorial

Pierre Pettigrew

Bill Graham

Immigration minister Judy Sgro grants work permit to Romanian stripper

Did Sgro solve immigration the problems of a pizza-store owner in exchange for free deliveries?

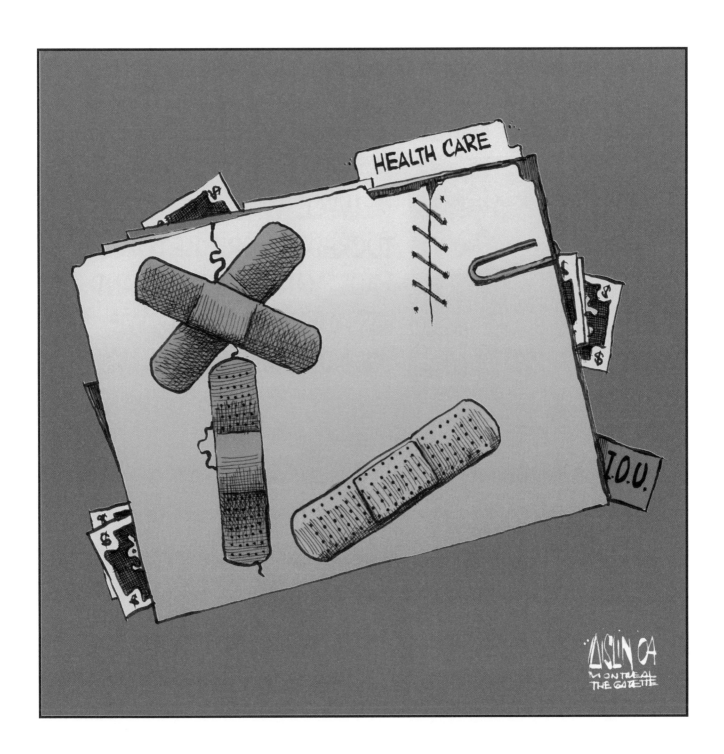

Questionable allegations of a Gagliano mob connection

NEXT WITNESS?

MY NAME IS BUCKY, AND I'M JUST ONE OF MANY RATHER EXPENSIVE SOUVENIR LIGHTERS THAT WERE PRODUCED BY A FIRM LOCATED IN ALFONSO GAGLIANO'S FORMER RIDING — AND WE WELCOME THIS OPPORTUNITY TO INFORM THE GOMERY INQUIRY EXACTLY HOW WE SAVED CANADA FROM SEPARATISM!

AISLIN 04
MONTREAL
THE GAZETTE

Where's Alfonso?

Gomery witness Jean Lafleur

Demonstrators moon the Gomery inquiry.

What goes around comes around

43

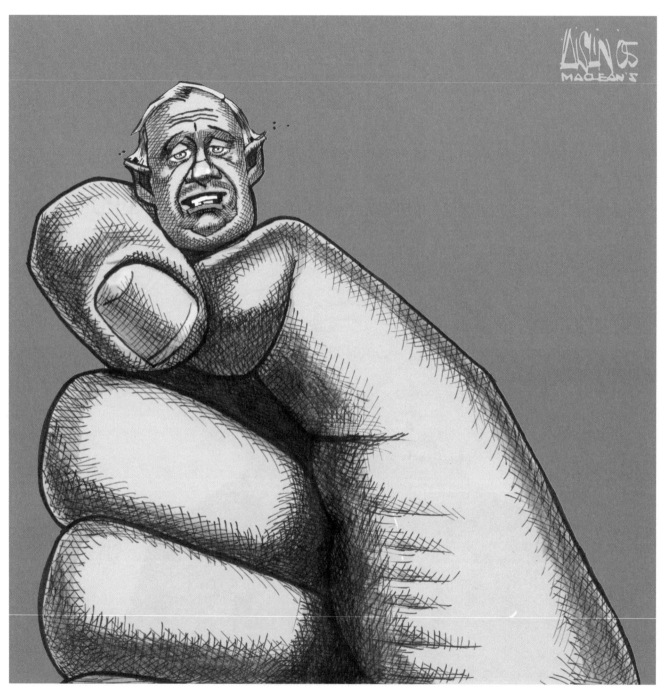

Election called for January 21, 2006

CHAPTER 4

Changing of the Guard

And so the nightmare continued for the Martin government. Each revelation from the Gomery hearings further eroded public confidence in the Liberals' trustworthiness. Canadians became exasperated with the lack of progress on major international and domestic issues.

The Prime Minister was forced into an early election when the House of Commons passed a motion of no confidence in November 2005. During the ensuing campaign, the Liberals tried to force the Conservatives' hand on social issues. The Conservatives and New Democrats trained their sights on the Liberals' ethical performance. Pundits prophesied and politicians blustered, but no one seemed to have any idea how the country would be voting.

The stalemate broke towards the end of the year. Opposition parties made hay out of an RCMP investigation into a possible leaks at the Department of Finance under Minister Ralph Goodale. The hue and cry was enough to push the Tories higher in the polls. Despite a few early campaign blunders, Canadians voted in January to give Steven Harper and his party a chance to govern, although by just the slimmest of margins.

As Paul Martin all but disappeared from the collective consciousness, Liberal leadership hopefuls made their first tentative declarations of interest.

And the new Prime Minister? He alienated the press, environmentalists and a little kid from British Columbia who grabbed the P.M.'s nose on national television! Harper also increased Canada's military commitment in Afghanistan, so the American government loves him.

Uh oh.

ITEM: STEPHEN HARPER LIKES THE BELGIUM MODEL FOR CANADA...

Unpublished.

Early campaign fumblings by Stephen Harper

Demands made that Ralph Goodale resign over income-trust decision leaks

AS THE LATEST CRAZE SWEEPS THE COUNTRY...

Tory numbers start to rise

A toe-curling read

Imagine, then…

DRIVING to the FINISH LINE...

PAUL MARTIN IN HIS LIBERAL RENT-A-WRECK...

Paul Martin moves on…

EVEN MORE LIBERAL LEADERSHIP HOPEFULS

...creating a log-jam to fill his job

Belinda Stronach chooses not to run for the Liberal leadership

Harper on a post-election Canadian tour

Harper on the world stage

Harper and the environment

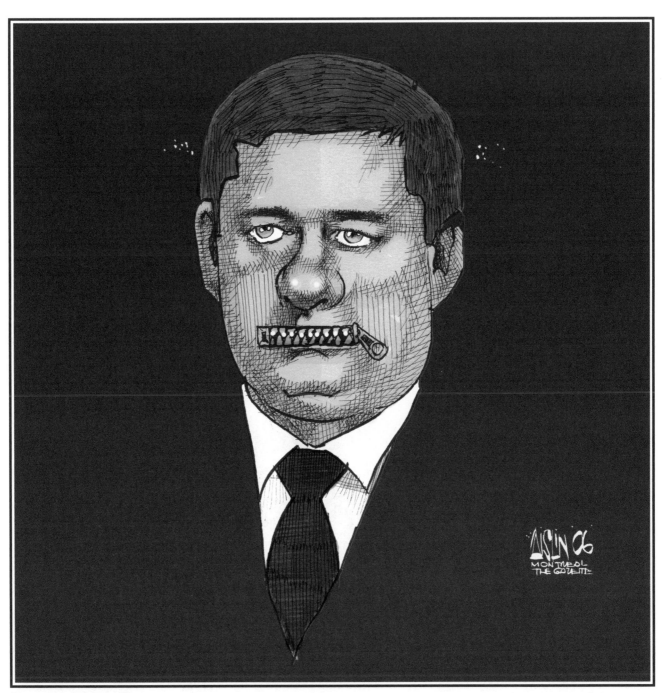

Harper and the media

Steve and Dubya

Commitment expanded in Afhghanistan

ITEM: U.S. EXPANDS WAR...

...ON CANADA GEESE.

CHAPTER 5

The U.S.
and Us

As a group, Canadians are strongly divided in their feelings towards the United States. Even individually, we can be somewhat schizophrenic on the subject of our American neighbours. Some of us cheer every U.S. initiative from the sidelines, cherishing only the warmest of feelings towards the world's superpower and its citizens. Another equally vocal segment of our population sees America – particularly under George W. Bush – if not as the great Satan portrayed by parts of the Muslim world, than as a troublesome bully.

The rest of us normally occupy an emotional middle ground between these two extremes, depending on the current headlines and on which side of the bed we got up. One day we may fume over the arrogance of American business lobbies and governments on subjects like 'mad cow' or softwood lumber and the next flood the American Red Cross with donations for Katrina victims.

'They' so easily become 'us'.

Riding a mad cow towards Crawford

Film *King Kong* is released

Troubles aboard the space shuttle Discovery

Katrina

George Bush's 60th birthday party

Montreal Expos to become the Washington Nationals

CHAPTER 6

Sports:

Lows and Highs

It's been feast <u>and</u> famine for Montreal sports fans over the past two years.

The open secret that the Expos would be leaving Montreal for Washington, D.C. was finally confirmed in September 2004. However, Montreal sports fans have always had to be adaptable: if we didn't have our Expos, at least we could cheer on Montreal's perennial favourite American League team, the Boston Red Sox. Our one consolation was watching the Sox finally win the World Series in 2005.

"Who, me?" We all got tired of the innocence feigned by athletes both pro and amateur when confronted with proof of their steroid use. Is there a sport that hasn't been touched by this lunacy?

Things went from bad to worse when NHL Commissioner Gary Bettman announced a lockout in February 2005, in effect cancelling the rest of the season as well as the play-offs. We were reduced to watching Gomery Commission hearings on TV.

NHL hockey finally returned to the arenas and not a day too soon. We got a much-improved game; we got Don Cherry back; AND the Leafs didn't make the playoffs. It was almost enough to make you forget the pain of the previous season. When the Canadian women's hockey team captured Olympic gold, the world seemed right again.

Like fans all over the world, Canadians flew their colours as they followed their favourites – and the politics – through the 2006 FIFA World Cup tournament in Germany.

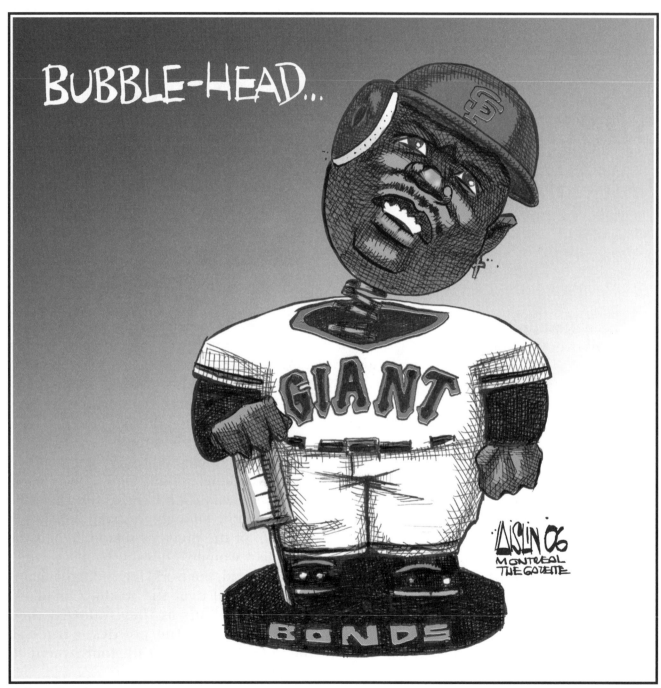

BUBBLE-HEAD...

...Barry Bonds

Red Sox win their first World Series since 1918

National Hockey League lockout

Liquor stores on strike

A long sportless winter

Hockey lockout ends

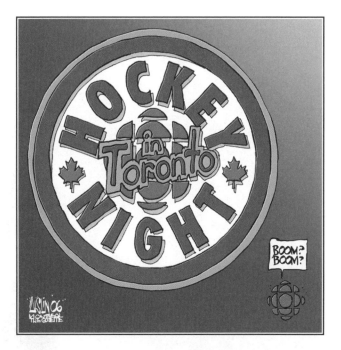

ITEM: DON CHERRY WILL PITCH PET INSURANCE...

OUR FAVOURITE HOCKEY PLAYOFF CARTOON THAT FIRST APPEARED IN 1997...

TORONTO MAPLE LEAFS

Leafs miss playoffs

IT MUST BE APRIL...

Annual April playoff madness in Montreal

reHABS...

Injury-plagued Canadiens

Canadian women win Olympic hockey gold

Canadian men don't win Olympic hockey gold

Changing allegiances during World Cup soccer

French superstar Zidane headbutts opponent

Grand Prix madness

CHAPTER 7

Ma Montréal

MAYOR MENTIONS THE "O" WORD...

Olympics for Montreal?

Despite losing the Expos, Montreal remains a fabulously vibrant and entertaining city. Its musical and sporting events bring in throngs of admiring tourists and are a source of pride for locals.

Not so the city's crumbling infrastructure, aptly illustrated by our world-famous potholes. There doesn't seem to be anyone who can get the notorious city workers – better known as les cols bleus – to provide value for our tax dollars. Despite these deplorable conditions, Mayor Gerald Tremblay was handily re-elected to a second term in November 2005. His unpopular opponent, Pierre Bourque, has since retired from the political arena.

Montreal's welcoming attitude towards newcomers is rapidly turning the city into a multi-ethnic, multi-racial society comparable to that of Toronto. This more diverse make-up is naturally moving the city past simple French-English squabbles, although there is still the occasional delightful dustup over signage.

Municipal election, 2005

Tremblay campaign poster

Westmount bows out of the Montreal super-city

Conservative Party holds a convention in Montreal…

...with much talk of Peter and Belinda

Montreal municipal workers slow down with little difficulty

A record number of West Island break-ins

THE BEST OF

Hip Hop
Blues
Folk
Reggae
Ethnic
Digital
Alternative

FESTIVAL INTERNATIONAL DE JAZZ DE MONTREAL

Soul
Gospel
Pop
Rock
New Age
Latin
Some Jazz

Karla Homolka released from jail…

…with rumours that she will live in NDG

Monkland Tavern ordered to become the *Taverne Monkland*

Alliance Quebec is broke

Daily Snooze

Québecencore!

Québec Québec Québec Québec
Québec Québec Québec Québec
Québec Québec Québec Québec
Québec Québec Québec Québec
Québec Québec Québec Québec
Québec Québec Québec Québec
Québec Québec Québec Québec
Québec Québec Québec Québec
Québec Québec Québec Québec
Québec Québec Québec Québec.
Québec Québec Québec Québec
Québec Québec Québec Québec
Québec Québec Québec Québec
Québec Québec Québec Québec
Québec Québec Québec Québec
Québec Québec Québec Québec
Québec Québec Québec Québec
Québec Québec Québec Québec
Québec Québec Québec Québec
Québec Québec Québec Québec
Québec Québec Québec Québec
Québec Québec Québec Québec
Québec Québec Québec Québec
Québec Québec Québec Québec.
Québec Québec Québec Québec
Québec Québec Québec Québec
Québec Québec Québec Québec
Québec Québec Québec Québec
Québec Québec Québec Québec

QUÉBEC!

QUÉbecEtc.

Québec Québec Québec Québec
Québec Québec Québec Québec
Québec Québec Québec Québec.
Québec Québec Québec Québec
Québec Québec Québec Québec
Québec Québec Québec Québec
Québec Québec Québec Québec
Québec Québec Québec Québec
Québec Québec Québec Québec
Québec Québec Québec Québec

Québec Québec Québec Québec
Québec Québec Québec Québec

Québec Québec Québec Québec
Québec Québec Québec Québec

QUÉ?

Québec Québec Québec Québec
Québec Québec Québec Québec
Québec Québec Québec Québec
Québec Québec Québec Québec
Québec Québec Québec Québec
Québec Québec Québec Québec
Québec Québec Québec Québec
Québec Québec Québec Québec
Québec Québec Québec Québec.
Québec Québec Québec Québec
Québec Québec Québec Québec

BEC!

"Québec"

Québec Québec Québec Québec
Québec Québec Québec Québec
Québec Québec Québec Québec
Québec Québec Québec Québec
Québec Québec Québec Québec.
Québec Québec Québec Québec
Québec Québec Québec Québec

QUOIBEC

Québec Québec Québec Québec
Québec Québec Québec Québec

CHAPTER 8

All's Quiet on the Quebec Front

Of late, Quebec politics have been a bit of a disappointment for editorial cartoonists. It's hard to sink your teeth into the kind of pro forma bickering the parties seem to think passes for political debate these days. As the level of angst in Quebec politics has subsided, so has some of the fun. The cliff's-edge excitement of the Lévesque and Parizeau years is missing.

Liberal Premier Jean Charest soldiers on despite his poor public approval ratings. He must be grateful that Parti Québécois leader André Boisclair is no more popular. Boisclair, who is openly gay, beat out party stalwart Pauline Marois for the PQ leadership at the party's November 2005 convention, despite his admitted use of cocaine while a cabinet minister in Lucien Bouchard's government. While Quebecers are reasonably blasé about this sort of thing, it is hard to predict whether these would be flashpoint issues in the heat of an election campaign.

There is one bright spot on the horizon for this cartoonist: Madame Louise Beaudoin is considering a return to politics.

Premier of Quebec – the toughest job in Canada?

Belly to belly

Development of Mont Orford park questioned

Will Philippe Couillard be Jean Charest's Dauphin?

Lucien Bouchard makes grand pronouncements on the state of Quebec

Gilles Duceppe decides not to run for the leadership of the Parti Québécois

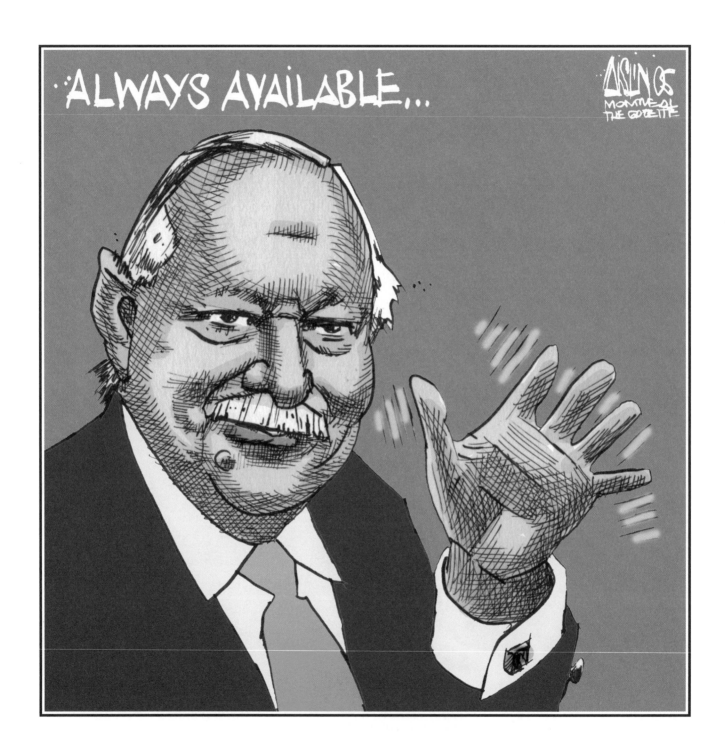

André Boisclair admits to previous "youthful" cocaine usage

PQ leadership hopeful Marois hopes to lose "stalwart" image

André Boisclair wins the PQ leadership

AND NOW, A QUEBEC POLL HAS A TICKET OF DAFFY DUCK AND TINTIN'S DOG, MILOU, HANDILY BEATING JEAN CHAREST AND ANDRÉ BOISCLAIR COMBINED.

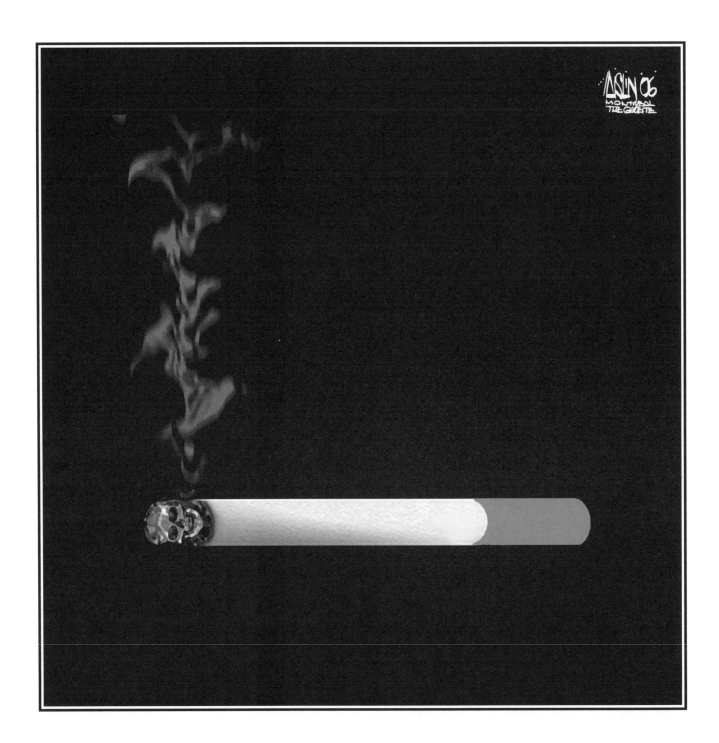

CHAPTER 9

Life
or Something Like It

When our friend Jack Rabinovitch turned seventy-five, he said: "If there's one thing I've learned, it's that when it comes to life, eventually you're going to lose. The trick is to lose slowly."

Now there's a philosophy that appeals to me! Yet as a professional observer of human folly, I see forces at work in the world that seem designed to accelerate our rush to the end. There are days when I would swear humanity is hell-bent on self-destruction.

Global warming – now there's an issue!

Our mind-numbing dependence on technology of all kinds is taking us down a path whose end is hidden from us.

Our children are obese. Our young people have developed an exaggerated sense of entitlement. Our cities are showing the cracks of unaddressed social problems.

We just allow ourselves to be swept along. Our adulation of entertainment 'celebrities' knows no bounds. We seem prepared to buy any product they're paid to push, embrace any cause they espouse. Every quasi-religious sect on the fringes finds its devotees.

We're losing quickly.

General Motors' financial difficulties

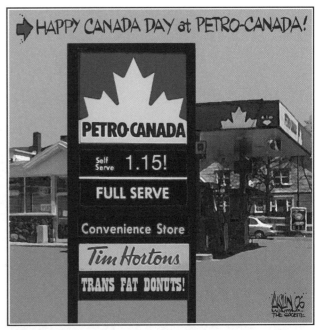

Aaargh!

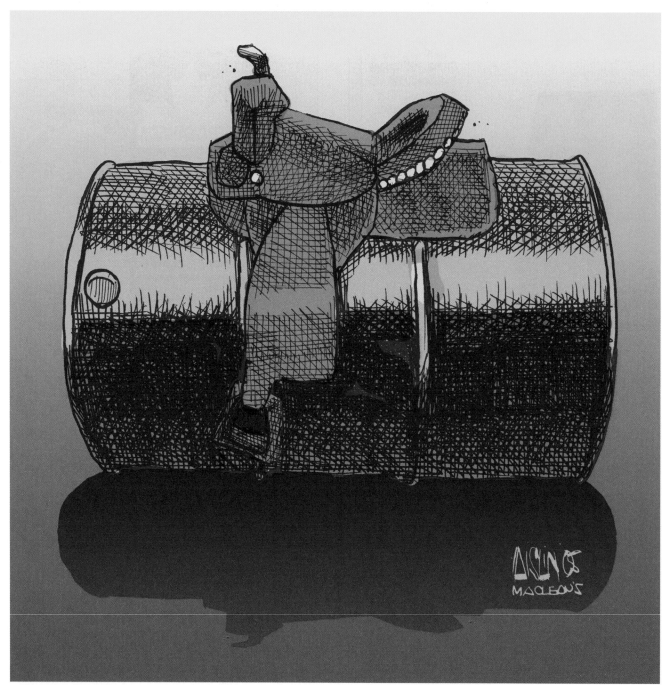

Calgary boomtown

Supposed Sasquatch tracks are found to contain bison hair

Unplugged

Where's the kitchen sink?

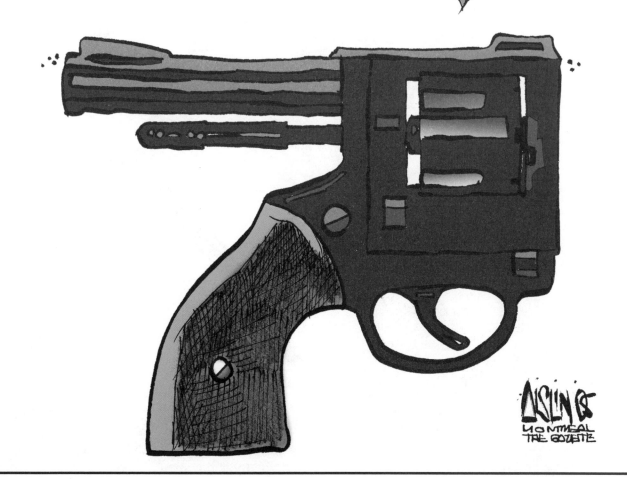

Academic moonlighting

Union drives thwarted

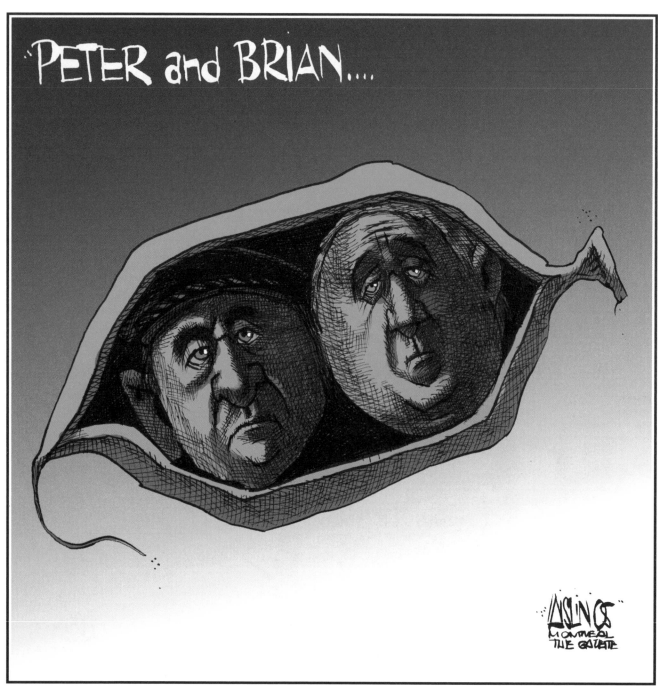

Peter C. Newman's controversial book of Mulroney tapes

Saving the seals

Céline Dion signs on to promote Air Canada

Michael Jackson's bizarre trial

Leonard Cohen is temporarily broke

Conrad Black's associate David Radler is charged with seven counts of fraud

Coming soon!

CHAPTER 10

A World

Run Amok

The world of the 21st century is a very confusing place. When Canadians venture out into the waters of international conflict, how do we set our moral compass? Everywhere we look, decency seems to be at a premium. The people we always thought of as the 'good guys' may be pillaging only on Tuesdays and Thursdays rather than every day. And the bad guys? Well, it turns out they've got a legitimate claim on our sympathy, too.

Sadly, there are evils about which there is no possible debate: children abducted as soldiers and sex slaves; violent racism and religious fanaticism; rampant but treatable deadly disease; profiteering at the expense of human lives; and there are so many more human ills that bedevil our world.

We arm ourselves with righteous indignation, but making things right often seems to be beyond our grasp. However our world was created, Earth and all its peoples are a grand experiment. I just hope we can figure out how to use the lab properly.

Garrison Keillor once said: "Have interesting failures."

What next?

Fidel Castro failing?

Kim Jong Il

Arafat dying

Mahmoud Ahmadinejad

Saddam Hussein on trial

Tony Blair

Queen will not attend Charles' wedding

Queen visits Canada during local political turmoil

London terrorist bombings lead to…

…immediate arrests

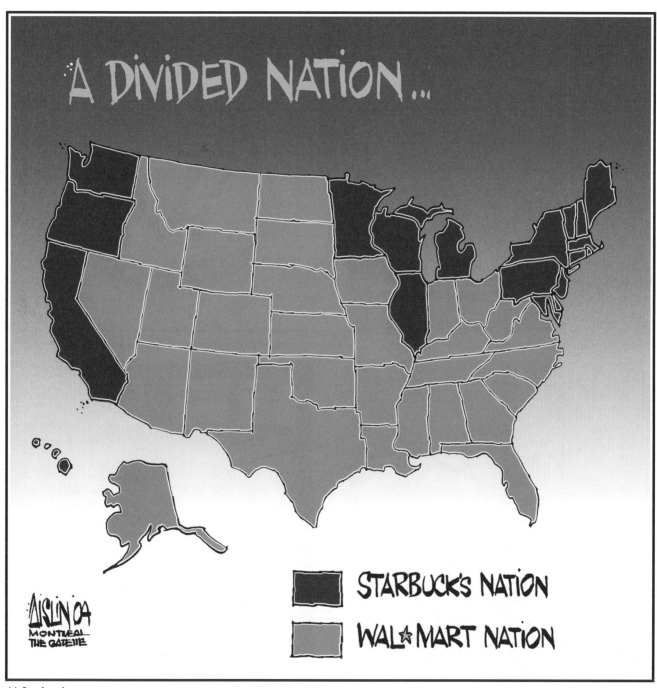

U.S. election

Bush-Cheney return to power

Cheney shoots an associate on hunting trip

European tour

Force-fed democracy

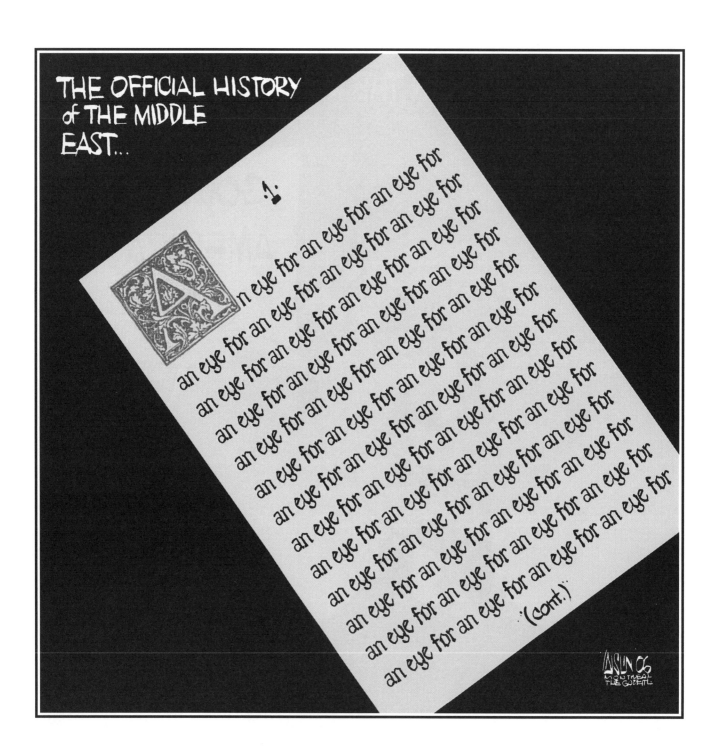

157

Condi Rice

Lebanese flag

CHAPTER 11

Cartoon Wars

Little Mermaid, Copenhagen

This brings us to the brouhaha over the twelve Danish cartoons of Mohammed. There is a great deal of urban myth around how this whole thing got started. What really happened, in a nutshell, is that in September 2005, a Danish children's writer was unable to find anyone willing to illustrate a book on the life of Mohammed. Concerned about the apparent self-censorship being exercised by creative people on all things Muslim, *Jyllands-Posten*, Denmark's largest newspaper, asked forty local cartoonists to draw Mohammed as they saw him. Not surprisingly, only twelve individuals actually responded and, in my estimation, rather timidly at that.

Nevertheless, as was widely reported, many Muslims were angered at these cartoons. Danish products were boycotted, embassies burned, churches destroyed and hundreds died in Muslim protests around the world. This overblown reaction was partly the result of orchestrated mischief by certain Islamist leaders at least according to eleven Canadian Muslim academics and activists in a piece that they wrote for *The Toronto Star*.

For a full discourse of my thoughts on this very important matter, please visit my web site at www.aislin.com where you will find the complete text of a speech that I delivered to The Ottawa Press Club on May 3, 2006 – the occasion of World Press Freedom Day.

In brief, the news out of the Danish kerfuffle has been both good and bad. The upside lay in the cartoonist's response: they collectively thumbed their noses at all the sound and fury. Here, I've included a selection of my favourite cartoons- drawn by myself and others – on the subject.

The unfortunate news is that press freedom suffered during this period. Most of our newspapers have been very nervous about this whole issue. Fine words were written, mind you. *The Globe and Mail*, in an excellent editorial, wrote that, "It would be tragic if the controversy over the Danish cartoons placed a chill on (cartooning) this most necessary of art forms." Nonetheless, neither *The Globe and Mail* nor an overwhelming majority of other newspapers would print the offending cartoons. They got out of the kitchen.

And what next? Will the nonsense continue? Will demonstrators in Copenhagen demand that the Little Mermaid clothe herself in a burqa?

And the horror continues with a terrible shooting taking place at Dawson College in Montreal.

Brian Gable, *The Globe and Mail*

UNE ARME DE DESTRUCTION MASSIVE?

Serge Chapleau, *La Presse*

Michael DeAdder, *The Halifax News*

Sue Dewar, *The Ottawa Sun*

Guy Badeau, *Le Droit*

Campus shooting at Dawson college in Montreal

Other books by Aislin:
Aislin–100 Caricatures (1971)
Hockey Night in Moscow (1972, with Jack Ludwig)
Aislin–150 Caricatures (1973)
The Great Hockey Thaw (1974, with Jack Ludwig)
'Ello, Morgentaler? Aislin–150 Caricatures (1975)
O.K. Everybody Take a Valium! Aislin–150 Caricatures (1977)
L'Humour d'Aislin (1977)
The Retarded Giant (1977, with Bill Mann)
The Hecklers: A History of Canadian Political Cartooning
    (1979, with Peter Desbarats)
The Year The Expos Almost Won the Pennant
    (1979, with Brodie Snyder)
Did the Earth Move? Aislin–180 Caricatures (1980)
The Year The Expos Finally Won Something
    (1981, with Brodie Snyder)
The First Great Canadian Trivia Quiz
    (1981, with Brodie Snyder)
Stretchmarks (1982)
The Anglo Guide to Survival in Quebec
    (1983, with various Montreal writers)
Tootle: A Children's Story (1984, with Johan Sarrazin)
Where's the Trough? (1985)
Old Whores (1987)
What's the Big Deal? (1988, with Rick Salutin)

The Lawn Jockey (1989)
Parcel of Rogues (1990, with Maude Barlow)
Barbed Lyres, Canadian Venomous Verse
    (1990, with Margaret Atwood and other Canadian poets)
Drawing Bones–15 Years of Cartooning Brian Mulroney (1991)
Put Up & Shut Up! The 90s so far in Cartoons
    (1994, with Hubie Bauch)
Oh, Canadians! Hysterically Historical Rhymes
    (1996, with Gordon Snell)
One Oar in the Water: The Nasty 90s continued in cartoons (1997)
Oh, No! More Canadians! Hysterically Historical Rhymes (1998,
    with Gordon Snell)
2000 Reasons to Hate the Millennium
    (1999, with Josh Freed and other contributors)
The Big Wind-Up! The final book of Nasty 90s cartoons (1999)
Yes! Even More Canadians! Hysterically Historical Rhymes
    (2000, with Gordon Snell)
The Oh, Canadians Omnibus (2001, with Gordon Snell)
In Your Face ... other recent cartoons (2001)
More Marvellous Canadians! (2002, with Gordon Snell)
The Illustrated Canadian Songbook, (2003, with Bowser & Blue)
Further Fabulous Canadians! (2004, with Gordon Snell)
OH,OH! ...and other recent cartoons (2004)
The Best Of OH! CANADIANS (2006, with Gordon Snell)